Portrait of
SEATTLE

 Portrait of America Series

Portrait of
SEATTLE

Photography by Ed Cooper
Text by Archie Satterfield

GRAPHIC ARTS CENTER PUBLISHING COMPANY
Portland, Oregon

Cover: Soaring Gothic arches and sparkling courtyard fountains, designed by architect Minoru Yamasaki, create an elegant entry to the Pacific Science Center.

Title Page: Every approach to Seattle, whether on land or water, creates a feeling of excitement; here, heading north on Interstate 5 towards the business district at night.

Acknowledgement: Page 40 photograph by Ed Cooper reproduced with permission from the Seattle and King County Historical Society, Museum of History and Industry.

International Standard Book Number 0-912856-56-4
Library of Congress catalog number 79-55980
Copyright © 1980 by Graphic Arts Center Publishing Company
2000 N.W. Wilson, Portland, Oregon 97209
Typesetting • Paul O. Giesey/Adcrafters
Printing • Graphic Arts Center
Binding • Lincoln & Allen
Printed in the United States of America

Lincoln Park offers 130 acres for exploration and picnics in forested areas, open meadows, and rocky beaches along Puget Sound.

From West Seattle, colorful, changing vistas of the city skyline and surrounding waters are brought to light with each movement of the sun.

Downtown Seattle, the Space Needle, and homes on the slopes of Queen Anne Hill rise in the distance above the southern shore of Lake Union.

Overleaf: Golden leaves are a sign of autumn in Woodland Park, one of Seattle's busiest picnic and play areas, with its zoo, theatre for children, and acres of sports fields

The glass curtain wall of a modern downtown office building reflects the nearby structures and the changing light of
days and seasons.

Contemporary sculpture, titled Changing Form, by Doris Chase serves as a frame for the Space Needle and the city in this view to the southeast from Queen Anne Hill.

Beautifully designed entrance to the Pacific Science Center leads to four buildings of exciting aerospace exhibits, star shows, Oriental puzzles, and Northwest Indian displays.

*Shaped almost like a flying saucer, the observation deck
and restaurant of the Space Needle rise over 600 feet above
Seattle Center, site of the 1962 World's Fair.*

Azalea Way is a main trail in the University of Washington Arboretum, a 260-acre nature wonderland of Pacific Northwest plants, shrubs, and trees.

14

Lincoln Park, with its beaches along Puget Sound, and groves of redwood, cedar, and fir, is just minutes from downtown Seattle.

Ships from all over the world sail into Elliott Bay creating
an intriguing international waterfront in the center of the
city.

SEATTLE
by Archie Satterfield

It rained most of yesterday, but the sky cleared just before sunset and off against the southern horizon we could see Mt. Rainier catching the last of the red evening sun. Today was clear with a cool morning. We built a fire in the fireplace and drank a second cup of coffee while watching the yellow of the morning sun filter through the trees. Later we sat outside, and someone commented on how hot it seemed after such a cool morning. Puddles of water circle the house, and the fir and cedar trees behind the house look fresh and green. It is autumn, but everything is still green and crisp as spring.

This could have been written in Seattle more than a century ago by one of the city's founders to relatives in the midwest. Many letters of the period carried similar paragraphs and sentiments. The freshness, the perennial green, the chill that seldom becomes frigid, the afternoon sun that warms without overheating, the feeling of immense space in spite of the tall, dense, dark timber — all are part of Seattle.

From Seattle you can see the saltwater of Puget Sound and the islands that step-stone across to the Olympic Mountains. Look in another direction, and you can see Mt. Baker hard against the Canadian border. Go to the twelfth floor of a downtown office building, and on a clear morning you can see three major Cascade volcanoes to the south: Mt. Rainier, Mt. Adams, and Mt. St. Helens.

Drive an hour in the summer, and you are in superb hiking country or ready to fish in a swift stream or preparing to take your chances in a kayak. Drive an hour in the winter in the same direction, and you are gearing up to downhill or cross-country ski.

Take a bus across town and you are on Lake Washington, a 30-mile-long body of water where sailboats, power boats, and tugboats share the clear water. A shorter bus ride and you are on the shore of Lake Union where houseboats for decades have peacefully coexisted with shipyards, restaurants, hotels, and seaplane harbors.

For one of the most dramatic visual thrills you can experience, take a boat ride on a clear, moonlit night around Alki Point, then toward Seattle, and watch the skyline unfold — from the Space Needle on the north to the Kingdome on the south. It is as if the city skyline was planned for such moments.

Seattle is a sensual treat. It is a city for the physically active. It is young, energetic, and clean. It has learned from other American cities, many 200 years older, to keep the city a pleasant place for people. The downtown section represents commerce. But those who conduct business there daily are accustomed to trees and flowers and tiny parks, places to help keep the urban existence in proportion, to remind them that living things other than people can survive in the center of a city.

Seattle is a baby sister among American cities because it was founded in the mid-1850s, long after many Eastern cities celebrated their bicentennials. But few other cities can claim as many original, positive factors as a foundation.

Its founders, the Denny party, were veterans of the Oregon Trail, as was nearly everyone in the Northwest by the 1850s. They arrived at Alki Point, tired and alone in the wilderness. Their dream was a common one: to come to the Oregon Territory where land was free and soil rich, and where diseases common to the midwest would not threaten one's health. The Denny party established a town, traded with local Indians, and cut timber to sell in San Francisco and other California ports. The floods of immigrants established hundreds of towns along the Oregon Trail and at its end. Only a few survived the first years, and Seattle was one of the few to thrive.

The Denny party named their dream city New York and originally located on what is now Alki Point in West Seattle. But the point was too exposed to the weather, and the sound too shallow there for docks. So the settlers moved around the mudflats to Elliott Bay and established another group of land claims along the bluffs that faced west on the bay, and named it in honor of a friendly Indian chief. True, the town site boasted many hills. But a good deepwater bay sat just below the bluff, offering more shelter from the infrequent storms that blew across the sound.

Gradually the site grew to be a major town on Puget Sound, and the addition of Henry Yesler's sawmill on the waterfront gave it an industry. This mill also led to the creation of a name for the central areas of American cities. Yesler built a skid for logs down the hill behind his mill, and loggers named it Skid Road. Westerners later absorbed the term into their vernacular to describe the slum section of cities where bums and alcoholics live, an alternative to the Eastern Bowery. To the chagrin of contemporary Seattleites, it is often misspelled as Skid Row.

Thirty years after the town was founded, Seattle was the major city on Puget Sound, in spite of stiff competition from Olympia, Tacoma, and Port Townsend. The founders used wood almost exclusively as a building material, as did other craftsmen of their day. And, as it did many cities, fire leveled Seattle.

Capitol Hill is one of the residential areas that rise from the shores of Lake Union.

Chicago burned, according to legend, because a cow kicked over a lantern. Seattle burned in 1889 because a cabinetmaker spilled boiling glue, or it boiled over, and started a fire that nothing could contain. In a matter of minutes, the flames spread throughout the business district, and by sunset that day the city was leveled.

The next morning, when city leaders gathered to discuss what to do about the smouldering ashes of Seattle, they expressed little defeatism and self-pity. Instead they decided to rebuild immediately, but this time in a different manner: the business district would be of stone and brick.

So Seattle grew again, and many of the buildings constructed in 1889 and during the next decade still stand in the Pioneer Square Historical District.

Probably few cities of its size have been rebuilt,

leveled, and rearranged more than has Seattle. The cross streets intersecting First, Second, and Third Avenues were so steep that steps were required on the sidewalks, and some people could not navigate them. Horses had difficulty climbing the hills, and, later, automobile owners found shifting gears almost as hard. This problem brought about the first of the leveling projects in the downtown district.

As the dirt was pushed and hauled and sluiced down to the waterfront, engineers used some of it to build better dock facilities on Elliott Bay. They used some to fill in the tideflats where the Duwamish River enters Puget Sound, and thus they created Harbor Island. But they left much of the dirt in the downtown area to level the streets, which created a strange situation.

As the street levels rose, the first floor of many business buildings became subterranean. At first, workers and visitors reached these floors by steps leading down from the sidewalk level. But because of debris tossed from the street down to the sunken sidewalks, the city eventually built lids with skylights so that people could shop in the naturally lit underground. Before long, merchants and landlords gave up and used the first floors for storage or basement rentals.

The leveling continued for years. Denny Hill on the north end of Seattle was the largest such project, and Seattleites still call the area the Denny Regrade. It runs roughly from Westlake Avenue to Seattle Center. This project caused great upheaval and, not surprisingly, resulted in numerous law suits. Some residents objected to the proceedings and refused to give up their homes and businesses. Photographs taken at the time show their houses perched precariously on pedestals of dirt accessible only by ladder. Construction workers based their engineering on a process learned by miners working frozen soil in the Klondike and Alaska. They used high-powered streams of water to sluice down the hills with the dirt which either washed into Elliott Bay or was hauled away by horse-drawn wagons.

Another major project was construction of the canal connecting Lakes Washington and Union with Puget Sound at Shilshole Bay. Seattle leaders accepted this proposal in principle, but the usual arguments followed over the location of the canal. One faction believed it should run directly from Lake Washington to Elliott Bay, ignoring Lake Union, and builders actually started the canal along the northern edge of Beacon Hill. But the backers went broke, and the Shilshole Bay route eventually won, with the locks at Ballard and a canal connecting the lakes near the University of Washington.

The University of Washington was originally downtown. It was later moved to its present site above Lake Washington, and many of its buildings were erected for the 1909 Alaska-Yukon-Pacific Exposition, Seattle's first successful experience with expositions. The next came 53 years later in 1962 with Century 21, the Seattle World's Fair that surprised everyone by making a profit. Many of the positive aspects of Seattle today are related directly to Century 21. It turned Seattle into a major city after decades of being a small, rather provincial town.

Since the fair, Seattle has remained in the forefront of the American consciousness. It has gained major league sports —basketball, baseball, football, soccer, and volleyball —and the basketball team, the Supersonics, became an NBA world champion. The fair widened Seattle's horizons and gave its leaders the confidence necessary to become a leader among cities.

For the average citizen or visitor, the most visual remnant of the fair is Seattle Center with the Space Needle, the Pacific Science Center, the carnival rides, and the elevated monorail that connects the center to downtown Seattle. Seattle Center is a successful attempt to provide something for everyone, ranging from those who like to sit on grass and look at fountains to the active who like to dance, go on thrilling rides, or attend concerts and plays. The Opera House has the excellent acoustics necessary for a major symphony orchestra and opera, and the Playhouse is the home of the Seattle Repertory Theater, a distinguished group of actors who perform the works of Shakespeare, Shaw, Miller, and other great playwrights.

Some of Seattle's parks are unique in the United States. One of the most original is the Freeway Park, actually a bridge over Interstate 5 that cuts through the center of Seattle's hour-glass figure. The city chose to enhance this midtown viaduct, using concrete as the principal material but softening it with imaginative landscaping and aquaducts. Planners call the park a bridge over a river of automobile traffic. The centerpiece is a magnificent fountain with waterfall that gently drowns out most of the freeway noise. The rest of the park is dotted with shrubs, flowering trees, and seasonal plantings and has enough places to seat a hundred or more brown-baggers from nearby office buildings and shoppers who drop by.

Another unusual park — so unusual that a major battle was fought over its construction and naming — is Gas Works Park on the north shore of Lake Union. It originally was a gas conversion plant, with storage tanks, boat dock, and miles and miles of pipe. When owners abandoned the plant, it sat vacant and dangerous to visitors for several years before planners came up with the idea of turning it into a park. So there it stands today, one of Seattle's most popular parks with a great view across Lake Union to the backside of Seattle's skyline. The equipment from the old plant remains, a monument to industry that has become a piece of modern art instead of a pile of rusting junk.

Another park came into being with the resurgence of the waterfront as a visitor destination. Not long after World War II, when freeways were becoming the automotive fad, Seattle's leaders decided to route one through the city. They built a tunnel beneath Battery Street, and it led to the Alaska Way viaduct, a

Princess Marguerite, a Canadian cruise ship, makes daily trips on the scenic waterways between Seattle and Victoria, British Columbia.

double-decked, four-lane freeway that cut off the downtown area from Elliott Bay.

In those days the waterfront was a working man's place. It made little attempt to attract visitors except with one or two seafood restaurants and a curio shop near the ferry dock. The viaduct caused no protest, and the waterfront remained unchanged until the late 1960s when interest began shifting from the suburbs back to the inner city.

Gradually the waterfront became more and more popular. A few excellent restaurants opened and survived; a motel-hotel was built out over the water; and developers turned an entire pier into a shopping complex with specialty stores and restaurants. Industry moved more and more shipping to the southern piers away from the downtown area, and the resurgence of the central waterfront was under way.

Although the noisy Alaska Way remains, it is no longer such a barrier, and the city decided to participate with private enterprise in making the waterfront a more interesting place. Planners drew up blueprints to build a park and a first-class marine aquarium. Both came into existence with a minimum of difficulty.

The park is visually interesting without being elaborate and is divided into several levels with fountains and plenty of places to sit and snack or to watch the gulls overhead and the boats on Elliott Bay. Nearby is a public fishing pier, and a promenade leads to the aquarium.

The snow-covered Olympic Range serves as a distant backdrop to the homes on Queen Anne Hill overlooking Lake Union.

The aquarium ramp takes visitors right down to the fish level; most of the tanks are beneath the bay's waterline. Sea creatures native to Puget Sound water live there, and many species are free to come and go as they please. Others obviously are captives of the aquarium and live in conditions similar to those outside the facility in Puget Sound.

It will probably be two generations before Seattleites become accustomed to calling the 400 acres on Magnolia Bluff, Discovery Park instead of Fort Lawton. After all, nearly a century of Seattle's history included an Army post on one of the city's prettiest pieces of real estate. The fort eventually became more trouble for the Army that it was worth, so the government deeded it to the city—broad beaches, steep bluffs, virgin timber, buildings, and all.

The city turned it into its largest park and gave part

of the land to Northwest Indian tribes for construction of a cultural center, Daybreak Star Indian Center, where craftsmen work and tribes hold meetings. Included in the new Discovery Park is a half-mile *parcours* for physical-fitness enthusiasts. Much of the park, however, has remained exactly as the Army left it.

Between Magnolia Bluff and the Waterfront Park is a long, thin stretch of land suitable for joggers, walkers, and sitters. Called Myrtle Edwards Park, it runs north along Elliott Bay from the Pier 70 shopping center.

A waterfront park of another kind is Green Lake, the portion of Woodland Park on the east side of Aurora Avenue. When its advocates first proposed adding Green Lake to the city parks system around the turn of the century, protest rhetoric filled the City Council chambers. Why, opponents asked repeatedly, would sane city fathers consider building a park in the middle of the wilderness? At that time it was almost an all-day trip by trolley from downtown Seattle through timber and bog to Green Lake. But its supporters held firm and the city acquired the lake and surrounding property.

Now, of course, Green Lake is hardly ten minutes by car from downtown. It is one of the most popular places in the Northwest for runners, joggers, walkers, roller-skaters, and strollers. Foot traffic is so heavy that the parks department has had to institute numerous rules about where one can run or walk or skate in order to avoid domino-like collisions. It is a foul day indeed when one does not see scores of crafts on the lake, everything from pedal boats to canoes, inflatables, sailboats, wind surfers, and kayaks. And there are few days out of the year, if any, that someone isn't swimming in the lake.

Of course, many other parks exist in the city, some rather basic in concept but with their own beauty that does not depend on manmade structures. Lincoln Park in Southwest Seattle is so large that even if the parking lots are full of cars, visitors still can find their private corner beneath the trees for a picnic or a walk along the beach.

Golden Gardens high above Shilshole Bay Marina is another beauty spot. Inland, with no vast salt or freshwater expanses to attract the crowds, are smaller and more private parks, such as Ravenna. And right in the center of Seattle is the grandfather of them all, Denny Park just off Denny Way with broad expanses of grass and native plants, such as rhododendron and azalea.

During the 1950s and early 1960s many Seattle residents succumbed to the national rage called suburbia, and, especially during the troubled 1960s, families packed up and headed out to the nearby towns. It looked as though Seattle was going to be populated only by low-income families surrounding the very wealthy in their exclusive enclaves.

But in the late 1960s and early 1970s, a pleasant thing happened in Seattle. Where the middle-aged, middle-class families vacated, young, energetic, and imaginative couples and individuals moved in. They took over aging but beautiful homes, restored them to their original condition, and soon central Seattle became a desirable neighborhood again. West Seattle, Beacon Hill, Capitol Hill, Queen Anne, Wallingford, and Fremont all emerged from what many thought would be ashes and rotten wood by the mid-1970s.

Along with this new interest in the center of Seattle came the demands by its citizens for certain amenities, including more living things in the city. So the city began a program of small, pocket parks. Almost any barren and unusable strip of soil became a park. If three streets angled into each other leaving a triangle too small for a building, it was a candidate for a few plants, some paving stones, and a bench. Other vacant lots owned by the city became P-Patches, small garden spots for residents to grow vegetables without having to dig up their own yard or for apartment dwellers with no land to till.

Other forms of self-awareness resulted. A city with an arm of the ocean at its front door surrounded on three horizons by mountains naturally has magnificent views, especially a city with hills such as Seattle's. Soon a series of small parks and viewpoints were noted and developed. Pieces of modern art adorned some of the viewpoints, and others remained in their natural state with only the addition of stable footpaths and benches.

Nearly lost among the files in the city records were various plans for Seattle's overall design. When these were unearthed, students of urban planning were amazed to learn of the impact landscape architects had on Seattle. The Olmstead brothers, sons of the famous Frederick Law Olmstead, designer of Central Park, laid out some of Seattle's most beautiful boulevards and parks. Although the city did not accept all their plans, they had an impact on the future planners.

Other plans were simply too ambitious or unrealistic. The Bogue plan, drawn by an engineer of that name, called for a system of boulevards reminiscent of ancient Rome. The main boulevard would have followed Dexter Avenue toward Puget Sound, then opened up into broad plazas with the public buildings and seat of county and city government overlooking the Sound. None of the buildings would have been taller than six stories because Bogue distrusted skyscrapers. He insisted that they were unsafe and offered proof that they were breeding places for malaria. In addition, they were impossible to heat, he wrote in the early years of this century.

In some ways, Seattle took nearly a century to realize what potential planners and dreamers had always known was possible. While a few were trying to make Seattle a people place, Seattle's leaders were more concerned with making it a place of commerce and were themselves content with living outside the city limits. That has changed dramatically within the last decade, and as much as any city in the nation, the city has learned that good living is conducive to good business.

The University of Washington has grown as rapidly as the city's major employer, the Boeing Company, and the university often is called the state's fourth largest city because of its more than 30,000 students and large staff. Like most large universities, many people know it only in relationship to its football team (which has made a few trips to the Rose Bowl, of course). But the university makes other contributions to the community that receive less attention.

In addition to the normal classroom work, the university is world famous for its medical school. It has attracted some of the finest minds in the world either as professors or as guest lecturers. The Philadelphia String Quartet was brought to the campus as permanent residents, even though the quartet keeps its original name. The university also sponsors a series of lectures and concerts, many of which are open to the public and free of charge. Residents tend to take the university's rich cultural contributions for granted; the city would be culturally impoverished without it.

Another example is the University Arboretum. A long, gracefully designed boulevard runs through the arboretum, and it is a mistake to drive along the boulevard, only occasionally glimpsing its contents. Numerous places to park lead to foot paths into the landscaped streams, rock gardens, and the formal Japanese garden. There are tiny waterfalls, natural pools, trees that virtually flame in the autumn, and scenes reminiscent of 19th century English landscape paintings. It is an incredibly subdued, peaceful place and one to which residents return again and again, simply to enjoy the beauty and the quiet. A big event for gardeners is the annual spring sale sponsored by the Arboretum Foundation where buyers can purchase native and exotic plants for their own garden.

Adjoining the arboretum, past the abandoned freeway project that residents fought to a standstill, is the Foster Island Nature Trail. Built by the Corps of Engineers and city agencies along Lake Washington, it is the channel for boats between Lake Washington and Lake Union. Until the trail was built, it was just another marshy area beside a lake. But now the path of gravel and planks allows people to stroll along the lake's shore in any kind of weather without sinking waist-deep in the bog. Planners added little turnouts for fishermen or sitters, and whenever a stretch of water had to be bridged, they made spans high enough for canoeists to pass under without bumping heads. The marshland area is popular with canoeists and kayakers, and many rent from the University of Washington's canoe house across the canal, which is called the Montlake Cut.

On the first weekend of May every year when the yachting season officially begins, this becomes one of the most popular areas for sightseeing. Almost every boat in the Seattle area joins a parade around Lake Washington, through the Montlake Cut, into Lake Union, and through the Ballard Locks. (Although everyone calls it the Ballard Locks, the official name is the Hiram M. Chittenden Locks, honoring a prominent engineer of the day.)

More than two million people visit the locks each year to watch the boats pass from fresh to saltwater, or vice versa. They also walk across the locks to the fish ladder where salmon, steelhead, searun cutthroat, and other species of fish enter freshwater. A visitor center stands near the entrance, and the Carl S. English, Jr., formal gardens are a few steps to the north. Species of plants from all over the world grow in the garden, and the grassy slope above the locks and waterway is a popular picnic spot.

Two decades ago Seattle had only one or two adequate shopping areas. Now the city has nearly a dozen major ones, plus little enclaves throughout the area. Perhaps the most popular is the Pike Place Public Markets that cling to a cliff between Pike and Pine Streets just below First Avenue. The markets are one of Seattle's most prized and protected institutions that date back to early times when farmers in the rich river valleys brought their produce to town to sell from stalls. Over the years, the markets changed, and in addition to food, fresh fish, and produce, strollers choose products from restaurants, gift shops, second-hand stores, charity stores, and craftsmen.

A proposal by the city several years ago to "improve" the markets caused one of the greatest uproars in recent history. The city wanted to tidy up the shabby markets and make them clean and sterile. Citizens almost uniformly fought this form of progress, and the city backed off. Now the market is restored and repainted, but the familiar delicious smells of coffee, teas, and spices abound, and vegetable, fruit, and fish sellers still noisily hawk their wares.

Citizens fought another long battle over the restoration and preservation of Pioneer Square. It began as the center of Seattle, but as the business district moved north and east, Pioneer Square became the prototype for Skid Roads. The city became interested in the area after a few businessmen moved in and began restoring the buildings. It was designated a historic district and public funds paid for the cobblestone park and other amenities in the district. Now Pioneer Square is a prime shopping and walking area, close to downtown, with excellent restaurants and boutiques. Since it is near the Kingdome, it is a hangout for sports and concert fans.

The Kingdome is another result of a controversy that divided the city and county for several years. Arguments did not involve the need to construct the buildings; instead they involved its location. Most people opposed to the downtown site now have come to appreciate the covered stadium. It is the home of all the major league sports in Seattle and close enough to the downtown area so that most fans have learned to take the free shuttle buses to the stadium rather than contribute to clogging traffic.

Another shopping place of special interest is on the northeast corner of the Seattle Center. When the Hansen Baking Company closed, developers turned the large brick building into a series of small shops and restaurants. In addition, nearby buildings also became eateries, making it a compact center.

Other pockets of specialized shopping can be found along Broadway and in the University District along University Avenue.

The newest such center is downtown in the Rainier Concourse, an underground shopping center that was built along with the new Rainier Tower at Fifth Avenue and University. The center, sometimes called Rainier Tunnel, runs beneath Fifth Avenue, with some of Seattle's biggest retailers represented in the shops along the way, and emerges on Sixth.

A waterfront specialty is the Washington State Ferry System. Rides across the Sound are always one of the highlights of Seattle visits. Ferries are the bridges across Puget Sound, permitting thousands of people to experience the pleasures of island living while working in the city. They connect Seattle with Bainbridge and Vashon Islands, and the mainland of the Olympic Peninsula.

They also provide the opportunity for people to get away from the city for a few hours. One of the most popular outings for Seattleites is to buy a picnic lunch at a delicatessen, take it aboard the ferry, and make a round trip to Bremerton or to Bainbridge Island. There are special low fares for walk-on passengers, and excursion fares are available that permit a few hours in Bremerton or in the other towns across the Sound.

Seattle is ideally situated for a series of one-day car trips to major attractions. You might want to spend more than a day on these trips, but if your schedule is tight, it is possible to see them in one long day.

Mt. Rainier National Park is everyone's first choice. On clear days it seems to loom so closely over Seattle that you think you can walk or ride a city bus to its base. Actually it is more than 60 miles away. But it remains the premier mountain in the state. At 14,410 feet it is the highest and the most massive and the most approachable because of the national park enclosing it. Its base and foothills are laced with hiking trails to match almost anyone's endurance capacity. There are overnight lodges and numerous car camp-

Mt. Rainier, a snow and forest-covered volcano, towers over Paradise Inn, a popular summer vacation lodge in Mt. Rainier National Park.

grounds. If you prefer to look instead of to concentrate on driving, bus tours during the major visitor months leave from several downtown locations.

Another great mountain experience is a visit to Olympic National Park across Puget Sound from Seattle. A one-day trip does not do justice to the park; two or three days is more realistic. Perhaps the most popular drive is from Port Angeles, where park headquarters are located, up to Hurricane Ridge. The ridge is at the timberline level with a picture-window view of the Olympic Range spread out across the western horizon. Hiking trails along the ridge provide better views and picnic tables among the sparse trees.

Or you can drive along the edge of the park by following Highway 101 out of Port Angeles. The road skirts Lake Crescent, considered one of the most

beautiful in the Northwest. The highway takes you along the edge of the park to the small logging town of Forks, then turns south and follows the coastal strip of the national park to Lake Quinault. This stretch of ocean beach is one of the wildest in the nation and one of the stormiest. If you enjoy rugged scenery with lots of offshore rocks and protruding headlands, this is an unforgettable trip.

The newest national park in the state is North Cascades National Park that butts against the Canadian border. It is largely wilderness and has few side roads. However, the North Cascades Highway is one of the most beautiful roads in the west. It climbs over two major passes and curves beneath sheer faces of mountains. Campgrounds are located along the route on each side of the park, but the park department allows no developments within the park boundaries.

Still another special area within driving distance from Seattle are the San Juan Islands. They are reached by Washington State Ferry from the small fishing town of Anacortes, 60 miles north of Seattle. The San Juans are composed of 172 islands, although most are little more than rock promontories. The ferry system serves the major islands — Lopez, Shaw, Orcas, and San Juan — and the route between them is one of the most scenic boat rides in the West. Visitors reach other inhabited islands in the group by plane or boat, and that is the way residents of these remote islands like it.

In addition to the San Juans, a daily ferry runs all the way to Vancouver Island in Canada, and another privately owned ferry makes daily trips to Vancouver Island from Port Angeles. Back in Seattle, Princess Marguerite, a steamship closely resembling a cruise ship, makes a daily trip between Seattle's waterfront and Victoria, British Columbia. The day-long voyage gives passengers four hours on Vancouver Island and is an easy way to see the very British city of Victoria, the provincial capital.

With such beautiful and mild surroundings in which to create, it is no surprise that the visual arts have reflected the prevailing blues, grays, and greens of the Seattle area, or that poems have more often than not dwelt on the misty and stormy shores, the foggy valleys, and the frequent rain. Both by accident and design, many elements of the Oriental culture, particularly that of Japan, have found their way into Seattle. Many homes and public buildings reflect Japanese landscaping concepts, in part because Japanese-trained landscapers have worked in the area for decades.

This preoccupation with things Oriental is not an accident. The prevailing weather that gives the region blues and greens and fog and moss lends itself well to the Japanese style of landscaping. Seattle has had a large Japanese and Chinese community since before the turn of the century, when they were brought here as manual laborers. Seattle treated its Oriental laborers no better nor no worse than other Western cities, until after the issue came to a head during World War II, when all Japanese-Americans were removed from the city to internment camps inland. After this act, later recognized as blatant racism, genuine efforts were made to atone for the previous treatment.

Seattle is very indebted to the cultures of the Orient and Europe. Although it is perhaps best known for its heavy concentration of immigrants from the Scandinavian countries, it was a great surprise to all when a survey showed that German is the major foreign language spoken in the city. Add to this a growing Samoan community, a large Chicano community, Filipinos, Vietnamese, and blacks, and the city has a great diversity of cultures.

The Seattle Art Museum houses one of the world's greatest collections of Oriental jade and Japanese and Chinese artwork in the Volunteer Park museum. Its Modern Art Pavilion in the Seattle Center contains important contemporary artwork, and the new museum being planned for the Westlake Mall downtown will be one of the first major museums to share quarters with shops and offices.

The city is famous for the Pacific Northwest Festival offered each summer by the Seattle Opera Association. The complete Ring cycle by Richard Wagner is performed in German and English, and opera buffs from all over the world make pilgrimages to Seattle for the event.

The Seattle Symphony Orchestra has always been in the front ranks of American orchestras, and it is a pioneer in taking music to the people instead of expecting people to come to it. An example is a recent tour the symphony made to remote villages throughout Alaska. Other tours are made annually throughout the state to small towns and public schools.

Another Seattle institution that continually amazes music lovers is the Seattle Youth Symphony, which holds its own with any professional symphony and draws teenage soloists from its ranks who are totally professional. But don't expect to walk up to the ticket office and buy a ticket the night of performances. It is almost always an SRO event, and the audience by no means is composed only of parents and grandparents of the performers.

Of course, Seattle has other forms of music. The Seattle Center management has avoided snobbery in favor of giving the public what it wants in the form of free concerts, especially during the annual summer Bumbershoot Festival. Here you will find some of the coolest jazz, hottest rock, and laid-back folk music available. Some of the talent is home-grown, particularly the specialists in folk music, due to the large number of people from the Eastern Seaboard and Midwestern hills who migrated during and after World War II, bringing their guitars, fiddles, and harmonicas.

All these amenities add up to what a city should be. It is difficult to fault a metropolis built in a mild climate with magnificent mountains surrounding it and lakes and saltwater on each side. While newcomers and some visitors complain about the overcast weather, others grumble about the heat, cold, and showers in Honolulu, Fairbanks, Phoenix, and Miami. Obviously the frequent rain and cool summer evenings are not for everyone. But those who learn to accept Seattle for the way it is, instead of for the way they would like it to be, also learn that there are few cities in the country, or in the world, that offer a comparable way of life.

The Smith Tower, built in 1914, serves as a landmark linking the historic Pioneer Square area with the downtown business section.

Overleaf: Old Seattle architecture contrasts with the new – in the ornamental detailing of brick and stone of turn-of-the-century buildings and the geometric forms of contemporary surfaces.

The varied materials, surface treatments, and design concepts of downtown buildings could serve as elements in an architectural stylebook.

Like Rome and Lisbon, Seattle was built on seven hills.
This view from Queen Anne Hill looks across Gas Works
Park and Lake Union to the University District and
Capitol Hill.

Denny Hall, named for one of the pioneer founders of Seattle, has continued in active use since 1894 when the University of Washington moved from Downtown to its present site above Lake Washington.

Colorful blossoms of flowering ornamentals create
springtime beauty in the University of Washington
Arboretum and in gardens throughout the city.

The beautifully landscaped campus of the University of
Washington maintains much of the feeling of the original
forested setting. Shown is Anderson Hall.

Daisies carpet a meadow accentuating the natural beauty of Seward Park, a forested peninsula extending into Lake Washington.

Overleaf: Mallard ducks rest in a quiet cove of Green Lake, a 340-acre public recreation center surrounded by homes.

33

The lovely faces of crocus blooms herald the coming of spring and the advent of fall in public parks and private gardens throughout the city.

*Snow, which decorates trees in Discovery Park, is seldom
seen within the city but offers year-round sports and
beauty in the mountains near Seattle.*

*Each season of the year brings new beauty and color to the
Arboretum's lovely and authentic Japanese Garden and
Tea House designed by landscape architect Juki Iida
of Tokyo.*

A marble ram from the tomb of a 15th century Ming
prince greets visitors to the Seattle Art Museum, known for
its Oriental art, rare jade, and collections of paintings
and sculpture.

39

*Old hand pump fire engines are displayed together
with a mural reminiscent of the Seattle Fire of 1889 at the
Museum of History and Industry.*

*All-wood flying boats were built in this original 1916
Boeing factory, now serving as a museum at Boeing Field
where today jet aircraft are assembled.*

*George Washington Memorial Bridge, spanning the waters
of Lake Washington Ship Canal and Lake Union, is known
to most Seattleites as the Aurora Bridge.*

42

Lake Washington Ship Canal, viewed from University Bridge, was dug in 1916 to create a huge fresh water harbor linking Lake Washington, Lake Union, and Salmon Bay to Puget Sound.

Fisherman's Wharf is home port for Seattle's commercial fishing fleet which works the Pacific Ocean from Alaska to Mexico, in search of salmon, halibut, snapper, sole, cod, and crab.

Brightly colored floats, stored inside the crab pots, ride the waves marking the location of the sunken traps used in catching the delicately flavored Dungeness crab.

Overleaf: A man-made breakwater, over a half-mile long, creates a safe harbor for more than 2,500 boats at Shilshole Bay Marina on Puget Sound.

Washington State Ferries, all named with Indian words,
offer delightful voyages for commuters and vacationers to
islands in Puget Sound and to communities on the
Olympic Peninsula.

*The golden glow of the sun dropping behind the Olympic
Mountains silhouettes a forest of masts at Shilshole
Marina.*

Fishing vessels of all types, including seiners, draggers,
trollers, and crab boats, can be seen at Fisherman's Wharf.

Twenty-mile-long Lake Washington, with its many forested parks on its shores, has been called "a mountain lake at sea level". The Olympic Mountains are in the distance.

*Floating concrete highway bridges replaced the old-time
Lake Washington ferryboats, but motorists still have the
feeling of traveling on the water.*

*The frosty touch of fall brings brilliant hues to the maple
leaves in the Japanese Garden.*

Alki Point Lighthouse has a beacon visible for 12 miles and is located just south of the beach where the Denny party rowed ashore from the schooner Exact in November 1851.

Built in 1881, West Point Lighthouse guides ships approaching the entrance to Lake Washington Ship Canal to the north and Elliott Bay to the south.

Overleaf: The fading light of the sun makes shadowy forms of Aurora Bridge and the marina, boat houses, and wooded shore of Lake Union.

Gas Works Park, created from an original plant site
on the north shore of Lake Union, includes much of the old
machinery in the landscape plan.

Spillways at Hiram M. Chittenden Locks control water levels, making it possible for freighters as well as pleasure craft to move to and from Puget Sound and Lake Washington Ship Canal.

*Seattle's huge, multi-purpose covered stadium, the
Kingdome, is close to the business center, Pioneer Square,
the International District, and the waterfront.*

The Kingdome is the climate-conditioned home for Seattle's professional teams: baseball's Mariners (shown here),
basketball's Supersonics, football's Seahawks, and soccer's
Sounders.

This towering waterfront sign calls attention to one of Seattle's most popular and picturesque attractions, Pike Place Market.

Fresh seafoods, vegetables, fruits, rare spices, imported delicacies, and vendors with intriguing accents give Pike Place Market the air and excitement of an international bazaar.

63

The elegant Victorian ironwork pergola, where people once
waited for street cars, is now part of the cobblestone park
in the carefully restored Pioneer Square.

64

Houseboats, along the shores of Lake Union and Portage Bay, display a variety of architectural styles, from flotsam-and-jetsam to expensive contemporary.

Freeway Park bridges Interstate 5 with flowers, green lawns, and flowing water to create a peaceful haven in the downtown business center.

The skyline of downtown Seattle has been pushed higher and higher in recent years by towering structures such as the Rainier Bank Building with its unusual pedestal base.

Naramore Fountain, along with other cascades, silence the
noise of thousands of cars traveling Interstate 5, beneath
downtown Seattle's unique Freeway Park.

Seattle is blessed with splendid views from vantage points throughout the city. This is from Kerry Park on the southern slopes of Queen Anne Hill.

The sun casts its light on Puget Sound and glows over the
Olympic Mountains in this vista from North Seattle.

Madrona trees along Magnolia Boulevard frame majestic Mt. Rainier seen in the distance above the Elliott Bay shipyards and harbor.

Overleaf: The image on the tranquil surface of this small alpine tarn along the Mystic Lake Trail gives no hint of the volcanic fire inside the 14,410-foot majestic Mt. Rainier.

A rainbow colors the rugged rock formations as the power-
ful flow of Snoqualmie Falls forms a mountain pool in the
north Cascades, only a 30-minute drive east of Seattle.

Mt. Rainier's broad shouldered silhouette is the result of
volcanic collapse and refilling with at least three major
eruptions occuring in the last 10,000 years.

The polar bear is one of the popular attractions at Wood-land Park Zoo, where more than 1,000 animals, birds, and reptiles are cared for in areas resembling their natural habitats.

Attractions at the Seattle Aquarium, located on the water-front, range from intriguing marine creatures to entertaining sea otters and harbor seals.

Through the stylized Gothic arches and the entrance to
Pacific Science Center one moves inside the building to
study the authentic designs of the doorway to a Kwakiutl
Indian ceremonial house.

The International Fountain at Seattle Center features
changing water patterns and music. The design by
Kazuyuki Matsushita and Hideki Shimizu of Japan was
selected in international competition.

An explosion of fireworks symbolizes the unique sparkle, excitement, and changing scenes offered by Seattle, the Northwest's largest city.